The Welland Canals Corridor
Then and Now

Four Canals at the Niagara Escarpment, c. 1928. Here, between Merritton and Thorold, the First Canal (lower centre) and the Second Canal (lower right) ascend the Niagara Escarpment. The Third Canal curves in a wide arc across the top of the picture, while the Fourth is under construction in the middle distance (with two pairs of the flight locks visible). (St. Catharines Centennial Library)

The Welland Canals Corridor
Then and Now

Roberta M. Styran and Robert R. Taylor
Colour Photography by Thies Bogner, MPA, FPPO
(Master Photographer)

Looking Back Press
St. Catharines, Ontario

Vanwell Publishing acknowledges the financial support of the Government of Canada through the Book Publishing Industry Development Program for our publishing activities.

Published by Looking Back Press
An Imprint of Vanwell Publishing Limited
1 Northrup Crescent, P.O. Box 2131
St. Catharines, ON L2R 7S2
For all general information contact Looking Back Press at:
Telephone 905-937-3100 ext. 835
Fax 905-937-1760
E-Mail vanessa.kooter@vanwell.com
www.lookingbackpress.com

For customer service and orders:
Toll-free 1-800-661-6136

Printed in Canada

10 9 8 7 6 5 4 3 2 1

National Library of Canada Cataloguing in Publication

Styran, Roberta McAfee, 1927-
    The Welland Canals corridor : then and now / Roberta M. Styran, Robert R. Taylor ; Thies Bogner, photographer.

Includes bibliographical references and index.
ISBN 1-55068-932-0

    1. Welland Canal (Ont.)—History—Pictorial works. 2. Welland Canal Region (Ont.)—History—Pictorial works. I. Taylor, Robert R., 1939- II. Bogner, Thies III. Title.

HE401.W4S793 2004   386'.47'0971338   C2004-902167-2

Cover photograph: **Thorold, 1998.** Tall ships wait to enter Lock 4 of the twinned flight locks, which "climb the mountain" (the Escarpment). One freighter has just left Lock 4, and another is being lowered in Lock 5.

Foreword

Public interest in the Welland Ship Canal has never waned since its construction during 1913-1930. Tourists and locals alike regularly line its banks to watch exotically-named ships in transit, or admire its mighty lock mechanisms at work. Heritage groups and local authorities have worked to preserve remnants of the three previous Canals, the first of which opened in 1829. For many years, the Canadian Canal Society has focussed interest on the Welland as the only major shipping canal among Canada's several man-made waterways. The 2004 World Canals Conference, held in St. Catharines, celebrated the 175th anniversary of the First Canal's opening. This book, presenting Master Photographer Thies Bogner's stunning colour photographs, is part of the ongoing fascination with Niagara's Canal.

For our part, we have spent over a quarter of a century scouring libraries, museums, archives and private collections in North America and Great Britain, amassing a unique collection of (mainly) black and white photographs dating back to 1860, as well as copies of early paintings, maps, drawings, and documents. Some of these have been published in our previous books.

This anniversary volume offers us a chance to picture the Welland Canal as it was in bygone days, in contrast with modern views, photographed by Mr. Bogner. Where it has proved impossible to match earlier views, we have included some outstanding photographs of selected sites, both historic and modern. We hope that this "then and now" perspective, supplemented by our captions, will engage the reader's imagination. A map showing the routes of the Welland Canals, and an appendix with basic information, including construction dates, number and size of locks, are also included so that the sites in the photographs can be pinpointed both geographically and historically.

In our previous publications we have acknowledged the many individuals, on both sides of the Atlantic, who have given us valuable encouragement and assistance over the years. This volume continues our debt to them. In addition, we are grateful to Thies Bogner, whose interest in photographing so many aspects of the Welland Canal over the past forty years has made it possible to present its modern face in contrast to its past.

The authors acknowledge the generous donations of Mr. L.R. (Red) Wilson and the Wilson Foundation, as well as that of the Niagara Marine Group. Their gifts have supported this publication and made possible the presentation of a copy to each of the delegates to the World Canals Conference 2004.

Introduction
The Four-and-a-Half Welland Canals

In the late eighteenth and early nineteenth centuries in Europe and North America "Canal Mania" seized entrepreneurs, engineers, politicians, and the general public. Practical men with visions of increased prosperity from improved inland transportation were not unknown in the Niagara area, but two were pre-eminent. On the American side, De Witt Clinton, elected Governor of New York State in 1817, was the driving force behind the Erie Canal (1817-25). "Clinton's Ditch" stimulated rivalry in Upper Canada, particularly in the mind of William Hamilton Merritt (1793-1862), a merchant of St. Catharines.

As early as 1818 Merritt and some of his friends surveyed a possible canal route, although actual work did not begin until 1824. Merritt hoped to interest the governments of Upper and Lower Canada (now Ontario and Quebec) in undertaking construction, to no avail. So he and his friends decided to "go it alone," obtaining an enabling Act for the Welland Canal Company, and opening subscription books. Ironically, although Upper Canada did later contribute substantially, it was financiers from New York City who provided most of the initial funding—and the first sod was turned on 24 November 1824.

While Merritt originally expected to have the canal in operation by 1826 it was not until 29 November 1829 that the first vessels were able to pass through from Lake Ontario to Lake Erie, to arrive in Buffalo, New York on 3 December. Chronic shortage of funds necessitated building the locks of wood rather than stone, and by the mid-1830s wear and tear (especially the ravages of Niagara winters) had left them in a sad state. Consequently, plans to re-build in stone were discussed. Unfortunately, the rebellions in Upper and Lower Canada in 1837-38 delayed the start of construction. The unstable political situation led to an investigation and subsequent report by Lord Durham, Governor General of British North America in 1838. He recommended that the two colonies should be joined together as the united Province of Canada. When this was achieved in 1841 the new government bought out the private shareholders of the Welland Canal Company, and turned management of the Canal over to a newly-created Board of Works. By this time the private company had already begun work on re-building what was to be the Second Welland Canal, and the work was completed under the jurisdiction of the new Board. The magnificent cut stone locks, and the aqueduct in Welland, were marvels to behold, the remains of which can still be admired both in Thies Bogner's photographs and on site. The Second Canal, completed in 1850, was not only "permanent" in that its structures were of stone but also, in response to the growing size of ships, it was considerably larger than the First. The increasing number of steam-powered vessels, however, caused problems in locking through, and it was not long before calls for yet another enlargement were heard. The impending Confederation of the provinces of Nova Scotia, New Brunswick, Quebec and Ontario (which became effective in 1867) delayed a decision. A Royal Commission report in 1871

St. Catharines, 1999. An upbound laker enters Lock 3, watched by spectators on the viewing platform, which is connected by a walkway to the St. Catharines Museum. To the immediate left of the lock is the weir structure, and above it and to the left are part of the pondage system of the Fourth Canal.

recommended a uniform, and enlarged, size for all the St. Lawrence canals as well as the Welland. (See map, page 13) Construction of the Third Welland was completed in 1886-87. Again, the structures were of cut stone, many of which still stand, as Mr. Bogner's photographs—and on-site visits—reveal.

Not surprisingly, as even larger and more powerful ships were entering the Great Lakes, work had scarcely been completed when agitation began for further enlargement, and creation of a "deep waterway" from the Atlantic to Lake Superior became a rallying cry from cities, chambers of commerce, and ship-owners, among others, on both sides of the Canada-U.S. border. By now the Board of Works of the early 1840s had become the Department of Public Works, which managed the Welland until 1879, when the new Department of Railways and Canals was formed. After considerable debate in the early years of the twentieth century, the decision to enlarge the Welland Canal yet again was made in 1912, and construction began in 1913. Work continued with increasing difficulty during the war years (1914-18), until it was halted at the beginning of 1917. After construction was resumed in 1919 labour trouble bedevilled the project through 1920. Underfunding was a perennial problem, too, but construction continued until the first ships were able to transit the Fourth Canal in late 1930, although the official opening was not held until 6 August 1932.

Navigation continued on the earlier canals on a limited basis at the northern end, through Port Dalhousie up to St. Catharines, and water from the Third Canal was used by various industries in the St. Catharines–Thorold area, for a number of years.

In the late 1950s dredging and widening of the channel were undertaken as the Welland was prepared to take its place as a key element in the St. Lawrence Seaway, which was opened by Queen Elizabeth II and President Eisenhower in June 1959. As in the past, the new waterway had not been long completed before further enlargement was being considered. In the late 1960s two sets of plans were produced: the first was to twin the remaining locks, but this was rejected on the grounds that it would merely pass more ships, and would not permit the larger ships then being built to enter the locks. The second plan, which is still on record in the headquarters of the St. Lawrence Seaway Management Corporation in St. Catharines, was to build an entirely new canal, with four "super" locks on a route east of the present channel. Part of that plan was to build a wider, deeper and straighter by-pass of the City of Welland, which in fact was done, and opened in 1973—the first half of a Fifth Welland Canal.

The Welland remains a crucial link in the St. Lawrence Seaway, which is jointly administered by Canada and the United States. In the early years of the twenty-first century the possibility of enlarging the entire Seaway is under discussion—so "Mr. Merritt's Ditch" may well see its fifth incarnation. No doubt Mr. Merritt, if he could see it, would be surprised at how his small canal has evolved. He certainly would be gratified that his "ditch" was thriving, nearly two centuries after his initial vision of a waterway to link the Atlantic (and the world beyond) with the heartland of North America.

Thorold, 2000. Tall ships in Lock 4, upbound for "Canal Days" at Port Colborne.

Niagara Peninsula, 1837. The bird's-eye broadside, (with Lake Erie at the top) lithographed and published in London, England, was taken from a survey made by W.R. Callington, an engineer from Boston. The artist's chief interest was not commerce, but the naval and military positions on both sides of the Niagara River at the time of the rebellion led by William Lyon Mackenzie. It is obviously based on an earlier map, since the extension of the Welland Canal to Lake Erie, completed in 1833, is not indicated. However, the drawing does show clearly that the Welland Canal was a response to both the problem of the Niagara Escarpment and the possibility of attack from the United States, providing a means of transport between the Lakes and well away from the frontier. (Metropolitan Toronto Reference Library: T-14981)

Routes of the Four-and-a-Half Welland Canals. Of all the canal-side communities only St. Catharines pre-existed the First Canal. From 1829 to 1833 the village of Chippawa saw canal traffic pass along the Welland River to the Niagara River. With completion of the direct route to Lake Erie in 1833, Chippawa declined, as Port Colborne became (and has remained) the southern terminus. (Loris Gasparotto, Department of Geography, Brock University)

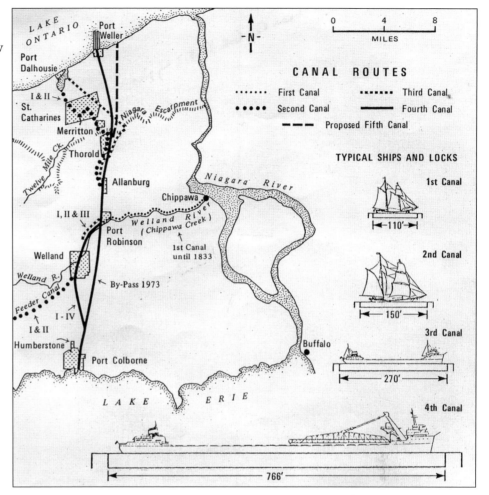

William Hamilton Merritt (1793-1862). The son of a United Empire Loyalist who emigrated to Upper Canada in 1796, Merritt served in the War of 1812, including time spent in captivity. His early business interests included a general store, sawmill, grist mill, cooper's shop, smithy, potashery, and a salt well. Need for a steady supply of water for his mills led to his interest in a canal, and in 1818 he and a few friends surveyed a possible line. While nothing came of that first attempt, by 1823 he was actively promoting a waterway to overcome the mighty Niagara Falls, and connect Lakes Erie and Ontario. Throughout his life he was a staunch supporter of, not only the Welland Canal and navigation of the Grand River, but also of a through route from the Atlantic via the St. Lawrence River. He was also an advocate of railways, steamships, and a bridge over the Niagara River. (St. Catharines Museum SCM: N-4101)

Niagara Peninsula, 2000. In contrast to the 1937 drawing (page 10) this satellite view shows tremendous urban expansion particularly in the Port Dalhousie-St. Catharines-Thorold and Welland areas. The routes of all four of the Welland Canals' main channels, as well as the Welland By-Pass have been highlighted. (September 1999, AIR-SAT Image Maps)

Direction of Flow ➡ from Lake Erie to Lake Ontario   Area 42 x 13km (26.1 x 8.1 mi.)

A Port Colborne	1 Break-wall at Port Colborne	6 Niagara Escarpment
B Welland	2 Wainfleet Marsh	7 Martindale Pond
C Thorold	3 Welland River	8 Queen Elizabeth Way
D St. Catharines	4 Short Hills Provincial Park	9 St. Catharines Museum and
E Port Dalhousie	5 Lake Gibson	Welland Canals Centre at Lock 3
F Port Weller		10 Niagara District Airport

Port Colborne, c. 1929. The entrance to the southern terminus of the Canal, looking north, with the government grain elevator at lower left, and the Canada Furnace Company at right, with two ships docked. Bridges 21 and 20 are prominent features, with Lock 8 (the control lock) visible beyond. (NAC: PA-48199)

Port Colborne c. 1996. The mid-1990s view, taken from further up the Canal, shows little remaining at the Canada Furnace (later, Algoma) site. The two lift bridges still dominate the landscape, and the remains of the control locks for the Second and Third Canals are visible to their left. Beyond, on the main channel of the Fourth Canal, is Lock 8, while the channel of the Third Canal winds around to the left, with the Robin Hood mill on its west bank.

Port Colborne, c. 1930. Widening of the channel for the Fourth Canal eliminated the small swing bridges (seen on pages 18 and 21), and replaced them with the two lift bridges, which carried Highway 3 and the Canadian National Railway over the present canal. At the lower right are the locks of both the Second and Third Canals. Bridge 20 was demolished in 1997. The government grain elevator (1907), and that of Maple Leaf Mills (1908), are prominent in the background. (NAC: PA-48202)

Port Colborne, c. 1995. Again, the modern view was taken from further inland, and includes the Robin Hood mill on Ramey's Bend of the Third Canal. The loss of major industrial activity on the east side of the harbour is apparent, but the stack of a major plant, the International Nickel Company (INCO), and the grain elevators remind us of Port's heritage.

Port Colborne, c. 1860. In the foreground are the winches and gates of Lock 27 of the Second Canal, with a characteristic white swing bridge. The Grand Trunk Railway's grain storage elevator is in the background. (Port Colborne Heritage Marine Museum, PCHMM)

Outer Harbor showing new Mill and government Elevator, Port Colborne, Ont.

Port Colborne, c. 1920. By this time the harbour at the southern terminus was being enlarged in preparation for the Fourth Canal. Coal is being loaded at the left, and several dredges are at work on the enlargement. In the background are the Maple Leaf Mill (left), rebuilt after an explosion in 1919, and the government grain elevator (right). Flour milling is still a key industry in Port Colborne and the huge mill and elevator are visible symbols of the role the Welland Canals have played in the city's history. (John Burtniak Collection)

Port Colborne, c. 1887. The two control locks of the Second and Third Canals, with East Street (demolished for Fourth Canal construction) and the Grant Trunk Railway elevator. Chain winches were used to pull open the lock gates, replacing the balance beams used on earlier canals. (William Koudys Collection)

Port Colborne, c. 1890. In this prosperous scene stores and businesses line the channel, facing the source of trade. West Street stores overlook the locks of the Second Canal (where the gates are shut) and the Third Canal (with its gates open). A typical swing bridge leads to East Street (out of sight, left). (AO: 13967-13)

Port Colborne, c. 1930. A laker stops at the wharf of the Canadian Furnace Company, later used by the Algoma Central Railway.
(John Burtniak Collection)

Port Colborne, c. 2003. Further inland, a sailing ship at the Snider dock reminds us that this area was once the flourishing East Street seen on page 18. Part of the stonework of the Third Canal lock is prominent in the foreground.

Port Colborne, c. 1910. Bunting-bedecked yachts line the west side of the harbour, waiting for their owners to take them out on Gravelly Bay and Lake Erie. In the meantime, the canal harbour provides a safe haven. (John Burtniak Collection)

Port Colborne. During "Canal Days 2000" that same area was temporarily home to visiting tall ships. Remains of the entrance lock of the Second Canal are seen in the foreground, reminders that such ships were once common sights passing through the lock.

Reichmann and Sons' Planing Mill, Humberstone, c. 1890. Another of the many mills which supplied construction materials for both the growing canal-side communities and export during the second half of the nineteenth century. All the staff (and presumably Mr. Reichmann's family) have been lined up for the photograph—but who is on the roof, and why? (PCHMM: P-980.8)

Reichmann and Sons' Planing Mill, now Frank's Home Building Centre, Humberstone, c. 2004. The company still operates on the same site, although the name has changed.

Welland, 1882. The Second Canal aqueduct, with the still surviving Court House in the background. Steam power had obviously arrived, and in the foreground (reflecting ever-changing technology) construction proceeds with another newer, and larger, aqueduct required for the Third Canal. (*Picturesque Canada,* 1882)

Welland, c. 1910. "The most stupendous piece of masonwork to be found in Upper Canada," an anonymous visitor noted in 1887. A freighter makes a smooth passage over the Welland River, with the Alexandra swing bridge (1904) open in the background. The Riverside Mill is on the left; the lock in the foreground carried canal traffic to the river. (Francis Petrie Collection)

Aqueduct, Welland, Ontario, Canada

Welland, c. 1937. The syphon culvert, designed to carry the Welland River under the canal in six concrete underground tubes, replaced the earlier aqueducts. The concrete structure may be less picturesque than the cut stone arches, but it was no less functional. (John Burtniak Collection)

Welland, c. 2003. In its turn the Fourth Canal syphon culvert was augmented by another syphon culvert when the Welland By-Pass was constructed (opened 1973). Today the walls carry cars and pedestrians to the park-like lands of Merritt Island (see page 39). The towers of the Main Street Bridge can be seen in the background.

Welland, 1986 and 1997. Less risky than swimming in the canal itself (a now-forbidden pleasure) was a dip in the swimming pool created in the disused Second Canal aqueduct. The "Cross Street Pool" was opened in 1946, and closed only in the late 1980s. The area has since been filled in and turfed over, but the magnificent cut stonework can still be admired. (R.R. Taylor)

Welland, c. 1910. A small construction shantytown called The Aqueduct came into being in 1829 where the Feeder Canal crossed the Welland River. The Feeder had become necessary to supply water from the Grand River to the main Canal. The small settlement continued to grow, becoming known as Merrittsville after 1842, and the county seat in 1855. Since 1858 it has been known by its present name, Welland. Growth was continuous until the 1930s Depression, and included construction of handsome public and commercial buildings along Main Street and, in the foreground, Canal (later King) Street. The Third Canal passes over the Second Canal and Third Canal aqueduct (at left), and under the Alexandra Bridge (foreground). (John Burtniak Collection)

Welland, c. 1965. The contrast between Third and Fourth Canal bridges is startling. So, too, is that between the modern lift bridge and the *Christian Radich*, whose passage drew crowds of admiring spectators, both locals and tourists. (John Burtniak Collection)

Welland, 1972. Various communities along the Welland continue to publicize their canal heritage. Here the Main Street bridge is floodlit to mark the last transit of a ship (the *Georgian Bay*) before the Welland By-Pass was opened the following year. (Welland Historical Museum, WHM)

Welland, 1972. Since then the bridge has been permanently in the down position, carrying only westbound road traffic, while a new concrete structure carries traffic in the opposite direction (see page 39). Thies Bogner photographed the floodlit bridge, just before the ship passed through.

Welland, 1928. The original channel of the Fourth Canal passed through the heart of the city. The raising of the bridges at Main and Lincoln Streets for the passage of ships became an increasing irritation as the amount of surface traffic grew after World War Two. (NAC)

Welland, 2001. Construction of the Welland By-Pass solved the problem, and the aqueduct and the Main Street bridge no longer serve their original functions. The curving concrete bridge at Division Street was opened in 1979.

Public Buildings, Welland

Welland, c. 1920 and 2000. From left to right, the Imperial Bank, the Weller Block and the City Hall, all overlooked the Third Canal—symbols of prosperity. Only the Weller Block still stands, although now very much altered. Since the opening of the Welland By-Pass the abandoned stretch of the Fourth Canal is used as a recreational waterway. (John Burtniak Collection)

Harbor Scene, Port Robinson, Thorold Township, July, 1920

Port Robinson, 1920. For nearly a century this community (at the junction of the Canal and the Welland River) was a focus of shipbuilding and, up to 1897, a port of entry. From 1829 to 1833, when the Canal was extended to Port Colborne, it served as the southern terminus. Its several hotels continued to provide a welcome break here at the halfway point between the Lakes, for the towboys and their horses as well as the ships' crews and passengers. Here we see dredges, a freighter, and tugs, suggesting a lively trade and commerce—long since vanished. (*Jubilee History of Thorold*)

The Deep Cut, 1914. The area between Port Robinson and Allanburg was known as the "Deep Cut," and ever since excavation began in 1825, it has proved troublesome. Disastrous land slips in 1828 forced abandonment of the original plan to obtain water for the Canal from the Welland River. Instead, a Feeder Canal was dug across marshland to bring water from the Grand River—crossing the Welland by an aqueduct. Despite considerable advances in technology since the 1820s, the first clearing for the Fourth Canal still required animal power to draw the "stoneboats," and men with picks and shovels! (NAC: PA 61103)

Black Horse Corners, 1928. This tavern, at a crossroads east of what became Allanburg, hosted a banquet following the turning of the first sod for the Welland Canal, on 30 November 1824. The lengthy speeches at the sod-turning are quoted in Merritt's Biography (p. 67), which continued: "After three cheers the company adjourned to the Inn, where a very good dinner was served by Mr. Beadgerley, to thirty-four gentlemen… After the cloth was removed, toasts were proposed and unanimously carried, when the company separated about dusk, highly pleased with the transaction of the day." The tavern has long since been demolished, its place in the history of the Welland Canal—and of Canada—almost forgotten. (SCM: N-7272)

Allanburg, 2003. When the area was surveyed in 1836, considerable growth was anticipated. By 1851, with about 300 inhabitants, it could boast two grist mills, two saw mills, two woollen factories and a tannery. By the late nineteenth century (with a population of only about 100) it was described as having "good water power… not utilized." Today, little remains of a once-flourishing settlement, but there is a cairn commemorating the turning of the first sod for the First Canal in 1824.

Neptune's Staircase, c. 1904. The most obvious of the many obstacles to water communication between Lakes Erie and Ontario (the Niagara Escarpment) was overcome by a series of locks, which carried both the First and Second Canals "up the mountain" on nearly the same site. "Neptune's Staircase" of the Second Canal is still to be seen in Mountain Locks Park in St. Catharines. This photograph, showing hand-operated gears above the sluices (or valves) in the gates, was taken when this stretch of the Second Canal no longer carried vessels, but still provided water power for several mills in the area. (AO—ST 406)

Neptune's Staircase, c. 2003. Water still flows through the series of cut-stone locks, but from the foot of the Escarpment it runs through culverts, to re-appear for a time in equally impressive locks which can be seen between Oakdale Avenue and Highway 406 (see page 67).

Near Lock 3, 1920s. During construction of the Fourth Canal, navigation had to continue along the Third Canal (cutting diagonally across the picture), with its large weir ponds and typical swing bridge (centre right). This exacerbated difficulties caused by landslides, which slowed the building of Lock 3 (foreground). Between Lock 3 and the new twin flight locks at Thorold (rising in the background) a lift bridge can be seen. Workers and engineers of the first three Welland Canals would have sympathized with their counterparts in the 1920s, for they had all faced the dangers posed by handling large volumes of water. (NAC: PA 43944)

Near Lock 3, 1997. In the modern view Lock 3 is just off camera lower left, but the flight locks and the winding course of the Third Canal are prominent. Third Canal pondage still serves its original purpose, while some of its locks are buried under Fourth Canal pondage east of Lock 6. When the Canal is un-watered for repairs during the winter, those locks can still be examined.

Thorold, 6 August 1932. The engineers (some with their wives) posed between two of the twinned flight locks of the Fourth Canal at the official opening, with numerous supervisors crowding the stairway. Alex Grant, who took over as Engineer-in-Charge when construction resumed in 1919, is seated centre front (between the two ladies in cloche hats). Grant, an irascible Scot, effectively supervised the completion of an engineering masterpiece. (WHM)

Thorold, 1994. Today the flight locks continue to pass ships up and down the Canal.

Thorold, c. 1925 and 2004. Today the route of the Second Canal is more or less under the road which runs across the centre of the picture. The Keefer Mill (extreme right centre) can be seen on pages 56 and 57. The Third Canal by-passed the town in 1887, and by 1925 the Fourth Canal was under construction. Mills along the Second Canal were in decline, since ships ceased passing through about 1915, and the water-way would soon be covered over. Thorold continued to prosper until quite recently as a paper-milling centre. (SCM: N-5285)

Thorold, c. 1885. The 650-foot long Grand Trunk Railway tunnel, over eighteen feet high, was separated from the water of Lock 18 of the Third Canal by less than three feet of earth. (NAC: C-20630)

Welland, 1978. There were no tunnels under the Fourth Canal, but when the Welland By-Pass was constructed several road and rail crossings had to be relocated. The Townline Tunnel in Welland carries both road and rail traffic under the Fourth Canal.

Welland Mills, Thorold, c. 1885. A business established by Jacob Keefer (a son of George, first president of the Welland Canal Company), this thriving grist mill was the largest such mill in the Canadas when built in 1846. The Second Canal, shown here, has long since been buried, but the handsome stone structure is currently undergoing restoration, for a mixture of residential and commercial use. (Edith and Bud Allen)

Welland Mills and Firehall, 2004. The new tile roof of the Welland Mills is apparent here. Both the Mills and the Firehall appear on page 53, and the Firehall on pages 60 and 61.

Thorold, c. 1886 and 2003. Another of George Keefer's sons, John, built this magnificent home, Maplehurst, on St. David's Road, around 1886. The delicate tracery on the porch no longer exists, but the main building is now being restored as an eleven-room inn. (Henderson's Pharmacy, Thorold)

Thorold, 1882. The artist's romantic view belies the industrial activity in the town. As early as 1825 Merritt's son had written: "Where the forest stood a short time ago, was now a scene of life and bustle. One hundred dwellings were on the summit [of the Escarpment], occupied by mechanics, labourers, tailors, shoe-makers, store-keepers and others." The 1882 view would have been taken from approximately in front of the Welland Mills (see pages 56 and 57). (*Picturesque Canada,* 1882)

Thorold, 2003. The towboys have long since vanished, and the Second Canal has been filled in, but the splendid firehall, built in 1878, has been restored for use as offices.

Merritton, c. 1910. The stately Town Hall (1879) and the hotel with its welcoming porch were results of a boom created by the industries along the Second Welland Canal. In the distance, at the curve of Merritt Street, stands the Beaver Cotton Mill (see page 64), one of a score of enterprises supported by canal water power. The section of the mill seen here burned in a spectacular fire in 1961. But the annexe to it remained, in use as storage for a number of years, then derelict, until recently restored as a popular restaurant (see page 65). The town's commercial viability endured well past the construction of the Third and Fourth Canals, both of which by-passed the town. Merritton and Port Dalhousie became part of the City of St. Catharines in 1961. (John Burtniak Collection)

Merritton, 2004. The Town Hall, which served as the St. Catharines Historical Museum for a number of years, has lost its turret, and is now a senior citizens' centre. The tall chimney of the mill can be seen in both views.

Independent Rubber Co. Ltd., St. Catharines, Ont.

Merritton, c. 1910 and 2004. In the 1850s a thriving industrial corridor began to develop in what became known as Merritton, where a series of fifteen Second Canal locks provided water power. Mills and factories were for many years a distinctive aspect of the area landscape. One such was the Independent Rubber Company factory, built in 1882 (originally the Beaver Cotton Mill). Only the annexe with its tall smokestack survives, still a landmark. (SCM: N-1077)

St. Catharines, 1987. Successive reconstructions have destroyed or buried the wooden locks of the First Canal. Today, only two are known to survive. Excavation of Lock 24 in the summer of 1987 provided a wealth of information for canal and engineering historians, and drew hundreds of spectators of all ages. Here a school group watches as excavators near maximum depth, exposing almost complete remains of the lock gates. The iron hardware was removed to the St. Catharines Museum, and the lock has had to be reburied in order to preserve the wood. (Welland Canals Society)

St. Catharines, 2003. The cut stone locks of the Second Canal have fared better. In addition to Neptune's Staircase, another series can be found, almost hidden under encroaching greenery, between Oakdale Avenue and Highway 406. There were for many years a number of mills and factories along this stretch of the Canal.

Merritton, c. 1860. The sawmill of Noah & O.J. Phelps (1855) was a typical example of the way in which pioneer industry was galvanized by the waterway. The Phelps brothers, related to the First Canal contractor, Oliver Phelps, were entrepreneurs who helped to create this industrial corridor. The locks, where the fall of water powered the mills, were tended by government employees. (SCM: N-1034)

Merritton, 2003. To ensure that reliable individuals would be attracted to the positions, handsome double stone locktenders' houses were constructed at intervals along the Second Canal. Two remain on Bradley Street, considerably altered, but still recognizable.

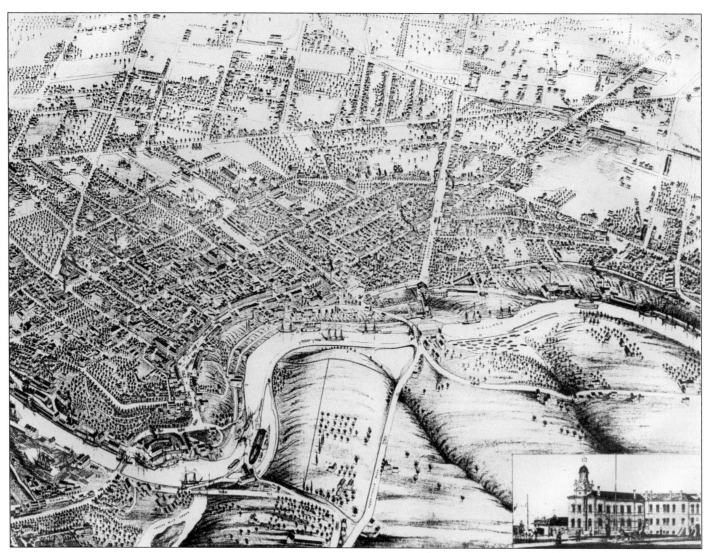

St. Catharines, 1875. Water supplied by the raceway, combined with pre-existing businesses, resulted in a concentration of industry on the St. Catharines–Thorold stretch of the Canal. The detail from a bird's-eye view was intended to promote both the town and its industries, which are shown located mostly on the north side of the Canal, since the towpath was on the opposite bank. The raceway is easily seen, running from the upper right and terraced into the hillside. Prominent enterprises along the canal are Shickluna's Shipyard, Drydock and Sawmill; Hunt, Cairns and Company Wheelworks; Norris' Wharf and Mills; Taylor and Bate's Brewery; Hutchinson's Mills; and the Dolphin Paint Works. (SCM)

St. Catharines, 2003. Today, much of the Second Canal through the city has been buried, and part of it is now covered by Highway 406. None of the industries of 1875 have survived, but Canada Hair Cloth, the red brick structure (erected in 1888) above the parking lot occupies the site of the Dolphin Paint Works. At the lower right can be seen Rodman Hall (see pages 84, 85).

St. Catharines, c. 1871. An obvious location for water-powered mills was near the locks, but this limited the number of mills and factories, hence expansion. Construction of raceways allowed other sites to be utilized. In fact, anywhere that the water could be passed over a mill wheel became a suitable location for a factory. The raceway here forked into two terraced channels, allowing construction of many more mills. Some industry has survived, although water power has given way to electricity. (DeVolpi, *Canadian Illustrated News*, 1871)

St. Catharines, 2003. The only remaining canal-side industry in this area is the Canada Hair Cloth factory. The Second Canal ran approximately ly through the left-hand arch of the Glenridge Bridge (see pages 90, 91), then curved in front of Canada Hair Cloth. The first level of the raceway ran behind it.

St. Catharines, c. 1864. Near Lock 3 of the Second Canal, both the "old" (a barkentine) and the "new" (a steam-powered canaller) are being constructed at the inner basin of Shickluna's shipyard. On the other side of the canalized Twelve Mile Creek can be seen Taylor's Brewery, comfortable homes on Yates Street (named for one of the First Canal's financiers), and the fashionable Stephenson House spa—signs of the city's prosperity. (SCM: N-2795)

St. Catharines, c. 1880. Not all the grain carried on the Canal was destined for flour mills—some was used for brewing. This site, across Twelve Mile Creek from Shickluna's shipyard, supported distilleries and breweries from 1834 to the 1930s. The schooner and scow were typical of the time. (SCM: N-4057)

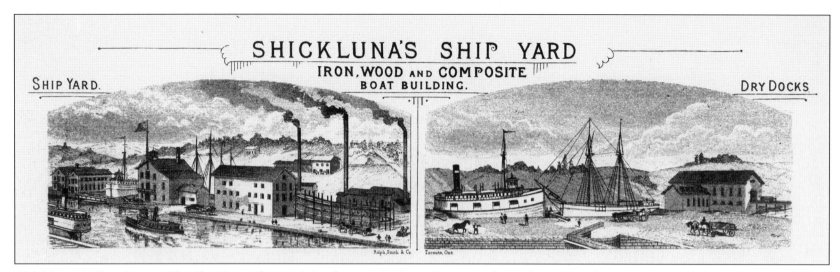

Shickluna Billhead, 1885. The Shickluna Shipyard, by then run by Louis' son Joseph, made sure its clients were well aware of its facilities. The views appear to be quite realistic. This yard was not the only one of its kind along the Welland Canal—although perhaps the best known. It is hoped that an archaeological investigation will be undertaken, as it is believed that the remains of a ship are buried in the area. (SCM: N-2798)

Shickluna's Shipyard, St. Catharines, 1894. By this time Shickluna's operation, one of the earliest shipbuilding establishments on the Dick's Creek section of the Canal, was in the hands of Frank Dixon and his son. The tugs *Charles E. Armstrong* and *Jessie Hume* are under construction. The first shipbuilder in the St. Catharines area had been Russell Armington, who sold his establishment outside Troy, NY, about 1825 and set up business on Twelve Mile Creek in 1827. Following his death in 1837 the yard was taken over by the Maltese, Louis Shickluna, who operated both it and a dry dock on Dick's Creek until his death in 1880. Between 1837 and 1880 Shickluna built over 100 vessels of various kinds. (SCM: N-2794)

St. Catharines, 1880 and 2004. Where once ships such as these were common sights, the water of Twelve Mile Creek now flows serenely past the site of Shickluna's yard, where area fire departments' men and equipment can often be seen practicing their skills on the pink structure. Steam is beginning to replace sail: the steam canaller *Persia* and the barque *Emerald*, built by Melancthon Simpson and George Hardison respectively, take on cargo. The *Emerald* was built specifically for the timber trade, and had stern doors which opened for loading. (AO: S-15995)

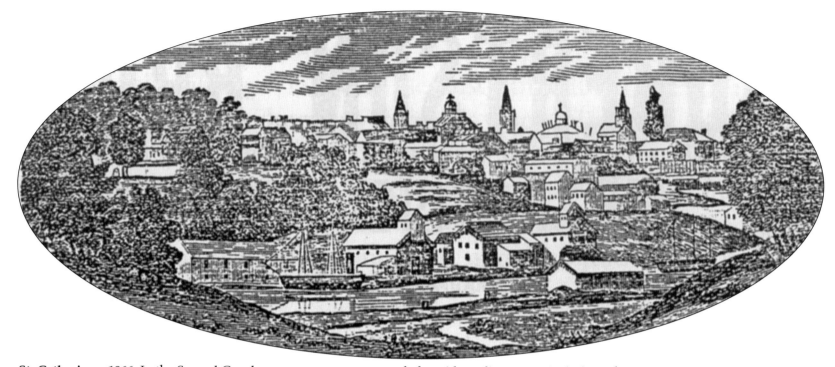

St. Catharines, 1866. In the Second Canal era newspapers commanded a wide audience, particularly in the growing canal-side communities. Many featured canal views, some owing more to imagination than to reality. This masthead from the St. Catharines *Constitutional* of 4 October is among the latter.

St. Catharines, 2003. The drab scene today is in marked contrast, with only the one industry remaining (Canada Hair Cloth, left) and a highway and parking lot covering the Second Canal.

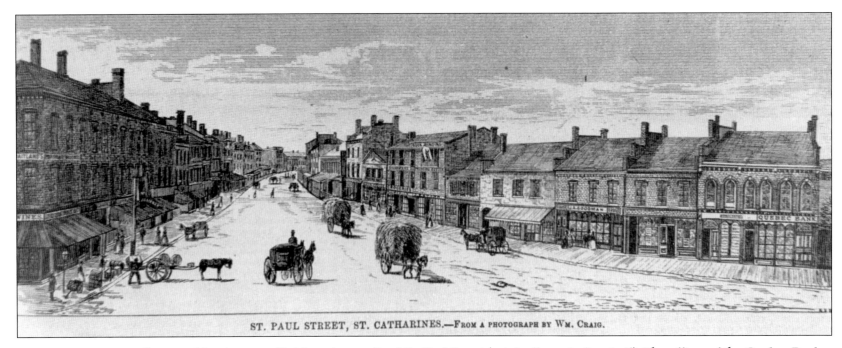

ST. PAUL STREET, ST. CATHARINES.—From a photograph by Wm. Craig.

St. Catharines, 1871. Shops and businesses of brick and stone lined St. Paul Street (originally an Indian trail). The offices of the Quebec Bank (founded 1818) suggest the sophisticated economic life being attracted by the Welland Canal. Many of the buildings on the right backed on the canal and its wharves. (*Canadian Illustrated News,* 23 September 1871)

St. Catharines, 2004. The view today is similar, although traffic was made one-way in 1954. While many of the buildings are new, behind some of the new fronts on buildings on the south side may still be found traces of structures in the earlier view.

Rodman Hall, c. 1865 and 2003. Some of the canal-side mansions which once allowed their owners to watch over the Welland Canal have disappeared. A few remain, such as this, built by Thomas Rodman Merritt between 1853 and 1863, which now serves as an art gallery. Recently taken over by Brock University, Rodman Hall increasingly hosts cultural events. Although it no longer overlooks the Second Canal it remains a lasting reminder of the area's canal legacy. (SCM: N-4962)

St. Catharines, 1876. The General and Marine Hospital was founded by Dr. Theophilus Mack in 1865, to serve injured or ailing sailors as well as local people. It soon outgrew it first home, a house on Cherry Street, and in 1870 moved into more capacious premises on Queenston Street, overlooking the Second Canal. (J. Lawrence Runnals, *A Century with the St. Catharines General Hospital*)

St. Catharines, 2003. Still located on Queenston Street, and now called the St. Catharines General Hospital, over the years it has grown far beyond Dr. Mack's imaginings.

St. Catharines, 1975. While the small houses built in the 1850s by Louis Shickluna for men employed in his shipyard were never intended to be particularly attractive, they were not unpleasing in their proportions. Not of great architectural interest, yet they were among the few remaining structures of the period which survived to the 1970s. But they, like so many other canal-related structures, have been swept away and, with them, a part of our heritage. (SCM: N-1559)

St. Catharines, 2004. New, up-scale residences, have replaced the workers' houses.

St. Catharines, 1916. While lift bridges are the most conspicuous of the Fourth Canal landscape features, other bridge designs were being used in the area. The first Glenridge Bridge, built in 1915 when the Second Canal (which it spanned) was still in use as a source of hydraulic power, could be a Roman aqueduct in southern France or Spain! Wear and tear of increasing traffic required its replacement by an earthen fill in 1955, and this was replaced by another bridge in 1980. (John N. Jackson)

St. Catharines, 2004. The photographer has turned his back on the earlier view, but the Second Canal is still there—buried under the highway. The Arthur Schmon Tower of Brock University is visible on the skyline.

St. Catharines, 1914. The Red Mill at Lock 4 of the Second Canal was a landmark from its construction in 1882 until its demolition in 1965. It was on the site of an earlier mill, built about 1828 at the foot of Geneva Street by Oliver Phelps, one of the contractors on the First Canal. It had a long history before being taken over by Packard Electric in 1895; later it was home to various businesses. (SCM: –7337)

St. Catharines, 2004. No trace of industry remains, the Second Canal is buried under the highway, and the bridge has been replaced by the concrete overpass. The only landmark is the spire of St. Paul Street United Church.

Port Dalhousie, c. 1920. The Third Canal's Lock 1 is at upper left; to its right, the imposing Consolidated Rubber Factory (formerly Maple Leaf Rubber, established in 1900), with Muir Brothers' Dry Dock still flourishing next to it. (NAC: PA-30556)

Port Dalhousie, 2003. An extensive marina has been built to the east of the Third Canal piers, and urban growth is apparent. The Rubber Factory is now occupied by Lincoln Fabrics, but Muir Brothers has gone. The Royal Canadian Henley Regatta is held on Martindale Pond, to the right of the island. The Third Canal cut through St. Catharines just above centre right.

Port Dalhousie, c. 1870. When the mouth of Twelve Mile Creek became the northern terminus for the First Canal, a thriving village sprang up serving and dependent on canal traffic. Several businesses, including Wood Brothers (centre background) and their on-site successor, Murphy's, specialized in ship provisions. A number of hotels and taverns catered to the crews, and shipyards built and repaired their vessels. (NAC: PA-14526)

Port Dalhousie, 2003. Today many of the old buildings have been renovated, and the area has become a tourist mecca. Port Mansion, prominent in the modern view, now caters to tourists and the boating fraternity. Recently an area consisting of the commercial core and a substantial part of the residential area in Old Port Dalhousie has been designated as a Heritage Conservation District.

Welland Ship Canal. Vessels in P: Dalhousie Harbour waiting passage thro' Present Canal. I.B.98. Oct:1928.

Port Dalhousie, 1928. The crowded scene in October 1928, as lakers waited in the harbour to enter the Third Canal, showed the need for yet another enlargement. Steamships predominate, but there are still a few masts of sailing ships to be seen. (SCM: N-1441)

Port Dalhousie, 2003. Now, a yacht club near Lock 1 of the Second Canal is crowded with recreational vessels.

S.S. DALHOUSIE CITY ENTERING LOCK 1.

"In the Good Old Summertime" 1910. What better day's holiday than to take the *Dalhousie City* from the Welland Vale wharf near St. Catharines, sail down Twelve Mile Creek, across Martindale Pond through Lock 1 of the Third Canal and, picking up passengers at Port Dalhousie, set out for Toronto across cool, breezy Lake Ontario? There is no longer regular steamer service between "Port" and Toronto, although there have been several attempts recently to restore this summertime pleasure. (John Burtniak Collection)

Port Dalhousie, 1960. At the annual Royal Canadian Henley Regatta on Martindale Pond (created by the Second and Third Canal weirs), six crews vie for first place. One of the last ships to moor in the inner harbour can be seen at upper right. (SCM: –1688)

Port Dalhousie, 1999. The course is still a popular venue, hosting a number of world class rowing competitions including the 1999 World Championships, seen here, and the annual Canadian Secondary School Rowing Association championships.

Port Dalhousie, c. 1885 and 2003. Group photography was still novel enough to draw out most of the employees of the Maple Leaf Rubber Works. The factory had opened in the former Lawrie Flour Mill: an example of how canal-side mills often changed ownership and function, and were renovated and expanded. Such changes often occurred after fires, but the mills continued to provide work for a small army of men and boys. Maple Leaf built a large plant in 1886: two buildings of five storeys each. A disastrous fire in 1899 resulted in another re-building. Lincoln Fabrics moved into part of the building in 1955, and now owns the entire complex. For another view, see page 101. (SCM: N-7470)

Homer (near St. Catharines), c. 1950. Congestion undreamed of by Merritt was common in the 1950s. Here, backed-up cars and trucks begin to move again after a twenty-minute wait while Bridge 4 was up for the passage of a ship. Traffic on the east-west Queen Elizabeth Way (Canada's first four-lane divided highway, opened in 1939 by Queen Elizabeth) rapidly increased with the post-World War Two boom, causing frequent bottlenecks such as this. (SCM: N-2339)

Homer, c. 1975. The solution to congestion in the St. Catharines area was the Garden City Skyway (opened in 1963), carrying east-west traffic on the QEW well above the masts of ships passing through the Canal. Queues at Bridge 4 are much shorter now, affecting mainly local traffic and visitors to the Shaw Festival at Niagara-on-the-Lake. Bridge 4 remains the only double-leaf rolling lift on the Fourth Canal. (Alfred F. Sagon-King)

Homer, c. 1970 and 2001. The *Pic River* is seen on its way south to Lock 3 of the Fourth Canal. It was equipped to carry either lumber and grain, or coal and iron. Here the 370-foot long ship, active from 1896 to 1978, is carrying pulpwood. The *Margaretha Green*, right, is also upbound. (Alfred F. Sagon-King)

Welland Ship Canal. Port Weller Harbour. Sept. 4. 1914

Port Weller, 1914 and 2002. Dredges, tugs, scows and steam locomotives brought tons of earth and rock to fill concrete cribs sunk into Lake Ontario, to create the piers for the Fourth Canal. Despite the massiveness of the structure, much of the west pier was smashed by a severe winter storm. Today the piers are firmly established, and provide shelter for ships approaching Lock 1. The Port Weller Dry Docks, on the east side inland from Lock 1, remains the only active shipyard on the Canadian side of the Great Lakes (see page 113). (SCM: N-1340)

Port Weller, 1931 and 1997. Lakers and salties await entrance to Lock 1 of the new (Fourth) Canal which, although not formally opened until August of 1932, was obviously urgently needed. The new northern terminus was named after John Laing Weller, who had been born in Cobourg, Ontario, and had worked on the Trent-Severn and St. Lawrence Canals before becoming superintendent of the Third Welland Canal in 1900. In 1912 he was put in charge of construction of the Fourth Canal. The Port Weller Dry Docks provide employment for a considerable force of skilled craftsmen, engaged in repairing and rebuilding a variety of ships. (Canada Department of Railways and Canals)

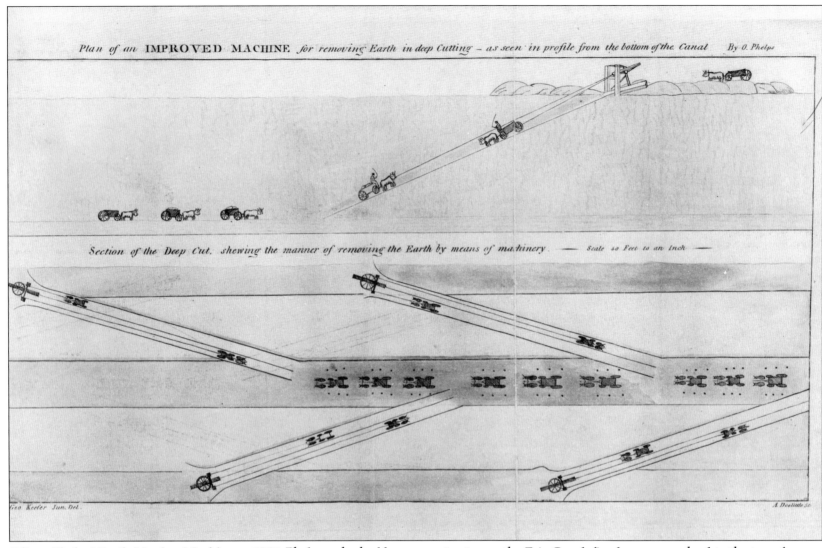

Oliver Phelps' Earth-Moving Machine, c. 1827. Phelps, who had been a contractor on the Erie Canal, fixed a wagon wheel to the top of a seven-foot post at the top of the canal bank. Then a rope with a hook at each end was fixed around the wheel, extending to the bottom of the channel. One hook was attached to a cart doing down, and the other to an already-loaded cart below. The weight of the descending cart helped to pull the loaded cart up to the top. Phelps (1779-1851), an American, settled in the area and founded a dynasty of mill-owners in Merritton. (NAC: C-101265)

St. Catharines, 1915. The site of the future Lock 2 with an up-to-date steam-powered shovel used in its excavation. The men with their carts and teams of animals used to haul away the spoil were still as important a component of canal building as they had been in the 1820s. (SCM: N-1001)

The giant device above was designed to remove stubborn tree stumps. The team of horses hauls a rope coiled on the central wheel; this turns the axle, tightens the chain, and uproots the stump.

Stump-Pulling Machine, Erie Canal, 1817-25. Many of the American engineers and contractors, who had taught themselves the skills needed to construct the Erie Canal, and who had also designed and built equipment necessary for specific tasks (such as this gigantic device), brought their expertise to help build the First Welland Canal. Without their knowledge, and that of Scottish-born Francis Hall (who had trained with the great British civil engineer, Thomas Telford), the task of transforming the dream of a canal across the Niagara Peninsula into reality would have been far more difficult, if not impossible. (R.M. Styran)

Welland By-Pass, 1970. The builders of the earlier Welland Canals could scarcely have envisioned the mighty equipment which would be employed on the Welland Canal By-Pass in the late 1960s and early 1970s. The scale can be judged by comparing the tiny figure of the man in the white hard hat with the drag-line excavator on which he stands—or even the truck at the right of the photograph. (St. Lawrence Seaway Authority)

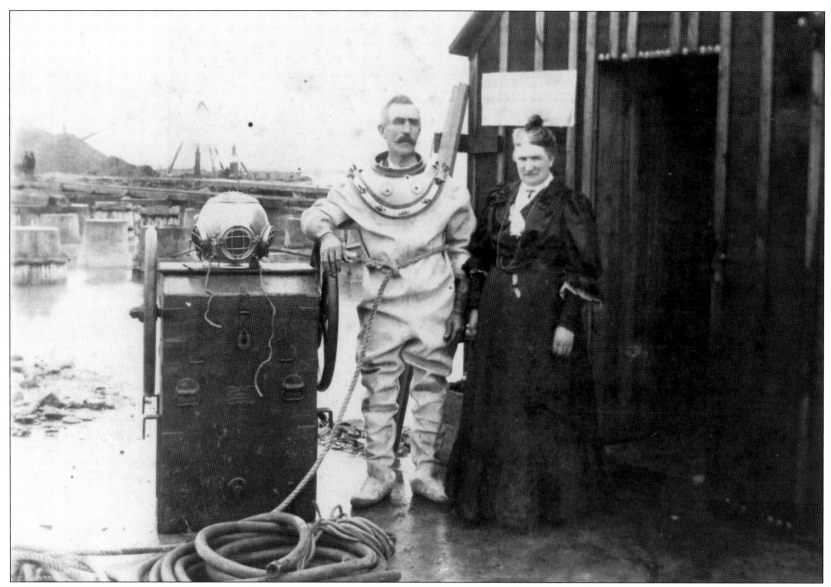

Welland Canal Divers, c. 1907-08, and 2000. Not all canal-created jobs were on or near the canal! Posing proudly with his underwater equipment (and his wife), Donald Fletcher of Port Colborne represents another technological development—improved ability to work underwater. His contemporary counterpart does similar work, but with even more sophisticated equipment, and far more stringent safety precautions. (PCHMM: P972-758)

Concreting, c. 1929. When construction resumed in the early 1920s after a war-time suspension, new types of equipment became available. The steel tower was about 150 feet (46 m) high, and ran on twelve wheels set on a 33-foot (10 m) gauge track. It was another example of the technological progress served and stimulated by the needs of canal-building. (SCM: L-1878)

Concreting, 1992. Repair work on the locks in the early 1990s indicates further advances in equipment.

Port Weller, c. 1930. The builders of the Welland Ship Canal took the public's fascination with the waterway into account, and planned to have parks and gardens along its length. This rock garden and greenhouse were part of a large nursery, itself to be an attraction. The Great Depression and World War Two terminated the project. All that remains today are the rows of trees planted along the channel banks to act as windbreaks. (PCHMM: P-979.16.475)

Port Colborne, 2003. Increasing realization of the value of attracting tourists to the Canal area has led to a number of initiatives in recent years. The viewing platform at Lock 8 has been enhanced by an attractive rock garden.

Third Canal, c. 1905. The boy in overalls, the son of a ship's captain, shows his landlubber cousin some of a sailor's skills on board a tug. Few canal-watchers are fortunate enough to actually board a passing ship today, since only larger motorized pleasure craft are allowed to share the waterway with the freighters and other canal workhorses—and the occasional cruise ship. (AO: Murphy Collection–4)

St. Catharines, 1994. The annual awarding of a top hat to the captain of the first ship through the Welland at the beginning of the season has become an occasion for celebration. Spectators line the viewing platform at Lock 3, to listen to the band and choir, and the speeches by various dignitaries.

At the Niagara Escarpment 2003. Locks of the Third Canal "climb the mountain." Lock 16 is in the foreground, Lock 17 is just beyond the railway bridge, and Lock 18 is at upper right. The locks are still used to channel overflow from the Fourth Canal, out of sight to the right. The gates of the locks are long gone, but the cut-stone walls are still impressive.

Appendix: Welland Canals Construction Dates and Dimensions

First Welland Canal: 1824-1833
15-16 Nov. 1824: first contracts
30 Nov. 1824: sod-turning at Allanburg
Jan. 1825: first payments to contractors
29 Nov. 1829: first ship through - **Official Opening**
3 June 1831: first contracts for extension to Lake Erie at Gravelly Bay
8 July 1831: first payments to contractors, Lake Erie extension
1 June 1833: first vessel through Port Colborne

- 40 wooden locks, 110 x 22 x 8' (33.5 x 6.7 x 2.4 m)
- maximum length of ship 100' (30.5 m)
- main branch draft originally 7' (2.1 m), increased to 7'6" (2.3 m)
- Feeder draft originally 5' (1.5 m), increased to 6' (1.82 m) by 15 May 1835
- water supply: Grand River through Feeder Canal

Second Welland Canal: 1840-1845
1 Sept. 1840: first payment recorded by Welland Canal Co. for "Bills of Work (New Works)," "Engineers salaries (New Works)"
1 Dec. 1840: first contracts by Welland Canal Co. for "New Works"
3 Nov. 1841: Board of Works contracts, deepen Feeder to 8' (2.4m)
30-31 Jan. 1843: first lock contracts entered into by Board of Works
21 May 1845: **Official Opening**, enlarged canal through Feeder to Port Maitland
22 May 1847: new Port Dalhousie lock, new line between Port Dalhousie and St. Catharines now in use; Feeder and main line now 8'6" (2.6 m)
7 June 1850: Welland Canal now fully completed to depth of 9' (2.74 m)

- 27 locks on main line, one each at the aqueduct, Port Robinson and Port Maitland, and two on the Feeder
- Port Dalhousie entrance lock 185 x 40 x 10' (56.4 x 12.2 x 5.05 m)
- other locks 150' x 26'6" (45.7 x 8 m)
- maximum length of ship 140' (42.6 m)
- water supply: Grand River through Feeder

Third Welland Canal: 1872-1881
26 Dec. 1871: contract to enlarge and deepen Port Colborne harbour
23 Jan. 1872: contract to further excavate the Deep Cut
9 Feb. 1872: contract to enlarge and deepen Port Dalhousie harbour
23 May 1872: first progress estimates submitted by Chief Engineer John Page for payments to contractors
11 Oct. 1872: contract for widening and deepening Feeder
17/18 July 1873: first contracts for various sections of enlargement
15 Sept. 1881: enlarged canal open for vessels of 12' (3.65 m) except at

aqueduct, where draft was 11'6" (3.5 m)

20 April 1882: **Official Opening**

May 1883: draft now 11'4" (3.45 m) to sometimes 12' (3.65 m)

1886: Annual Report for this year is first indication 12' (3.65 m) draft throughout (i.e., new aqueduct finished)

3 March-28 Sept. 1886: contracts to deepen to 14' (4.3 m)

26 May 1887: canal now open to 14' (4.3 m)

- 26 locks on main line, 270 x 45' (82.3 x 13.7 m); one each at the aqueduct, Port Robinson and Port Maitland, and two on the Feeder
- maximum length of ship 255' (77.7 m)
- water supply: obtained from Lake Erie

Welland Ship Canal (Fourth Canal): 1913-1930

30 Aug. 1913: contract for Section 1; 4 Oct. contract for Sect. 3

22 Dec. 1913: contract for Sect. 5; 31 Dec. contract for Sect. 2

2 Oct. 1914: contract for Sect. 4A

27 November 1916: decision taken to suspend construction for the duration of the war, effective at the end of the 1916 season

Jan. 1919: contracts re-let to original contractors after wartime suspension

27 Feb. 1924: contract for Sect. 8; 30 Dec. contract for Sect. 7

12 Oct. 1926: contract for Sect. 6

28 July 1926: contract for Sect. 4B

22 Nov. 1930: first vessel through, draft of 18' (5.48 m)

1931: ship capacity increased from 450' to 550' (137.1 to 167.6 m) x 18' (5.48 m)

6 Aug. 1932: **Official Opening**, for vessels 550' (167.6 m), draft 21' (6.4 m)

1933: ship capacity now for ships of 700' (213.3 m), draft 23'6" (7 m); draft increased to 25' (7.6 m) in 1935

1954 on: in preparation for St. Lawrence Seaway, deepened to 27' (8.22 m)

- 7 locks 859' (261.8 m); 766' (233.5 m) from breast wall to gate fender, beam 80' (24.4 m) with 30' (9.1 m) of water over the sills
- Port Colborne control lock 1380 x 80' (420.6 x 24.4 m)
- original maximum length of ship 730' (222.5 m); by 1998, 740' (225.5 m)
- water supply: Lake Erie

Back cover: **St. Catharines, 1995.** Looking north from Lock 7.